FRIEDRICH SEITZ

Student Concerto No. 2

for Viola in the First Position

with Piano Accompaniment

Opus 13

Adapted from
the original Violin Concerto
and edited by

SAMUEL LIFSCHEY

Associated Music Publishers, Inc.

DISTRIBUTED BY

HAL•LEONARD®
CORPORATION
7777 W. BLUEMOUND RD. P.O. BOX 13819 MILWAUKEE, WI 53213

Student Concerto No. 2

*Adapted from the original
Violin Concerio and edited
by Samuel Lifschey*

Friedrich Seitz, Op. 13

Tempo I°

ff

Tutti

ff

mf

rit.

ff

rit.

p

Adagio

p sostenuto

p sostenuto

VIOLA

FRIEDRICH SEITZ

Student Concerto No. 2

for Viola in the First Position

with Piano Accompaniment

Opus 13

Adapted from
the original Violin Concerto
and edited by

SAMUEL LIFSCHEY

Associated Music Publishers, Inc.

DISTRIBUTED BY

7777 W. BLUEMOUND RD. P.O. BOX 13819 MILWAUKEE, WI 53213

Student Concerto No. 2

Adapted from the original
Violin Concerto and edited
by Samuel Lifschey

Friedrich Seitz, Op. 13

VIOLA

Note: Optional fingerings appear in parentheses
⊓ = Down bow, V = Up bow.

VIOLA

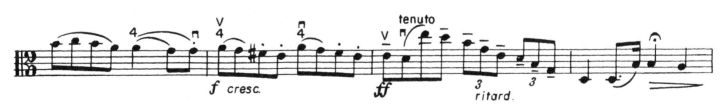

VIOLA

* The "F" is in the original version. If the fourth finger - extension is not feasible,
play the "B" instead.

Allegretto moderato

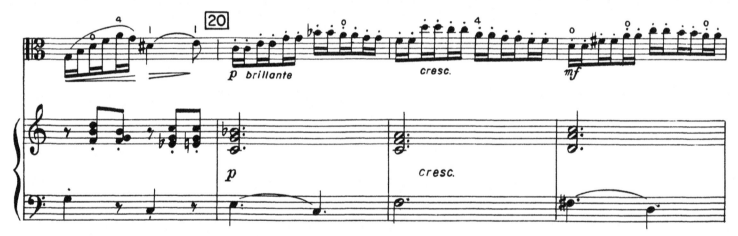